THE MANY SHADES OF BROWN
AND THE POWER IT HOLDS.
IN EVERY SINGLE TONE,
THERE'S A STORY TO BE TOLD.

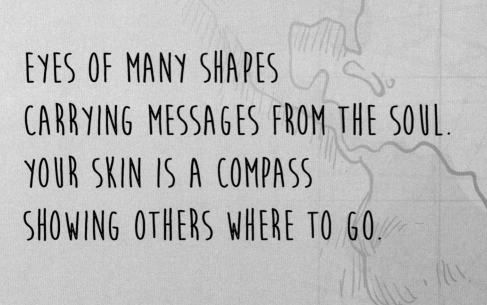

Eyes of many shapes
carrying messages from the soul.
Your skin is a compass
showing others where to go.

My sisters, my brothers:
shades of bronze and gold.
We stick together
as our shades unfold.

As brown as sugar cookies
or brownies you bake.
From peanut butter truffles
to dark chocolate cake.

Skin kissed by the sun.
As dark as brown can be.
As beautiful as the sky
when it reflects from the sea.

TIME AND TIME AGAIN
YOUR SKIN REVEALS ITS MAGIC.
JUST LIKE THE OCEAN,
YOU WERE GRACEFULLY CRAFTED.

SKIN THAT TELLS STORIES TO THE STARS
AND TELLS THE MOON GOODNIGHT.
IT SENDS PEACEFUL ENERGY
ALL DAY AND ALL NIGHT.

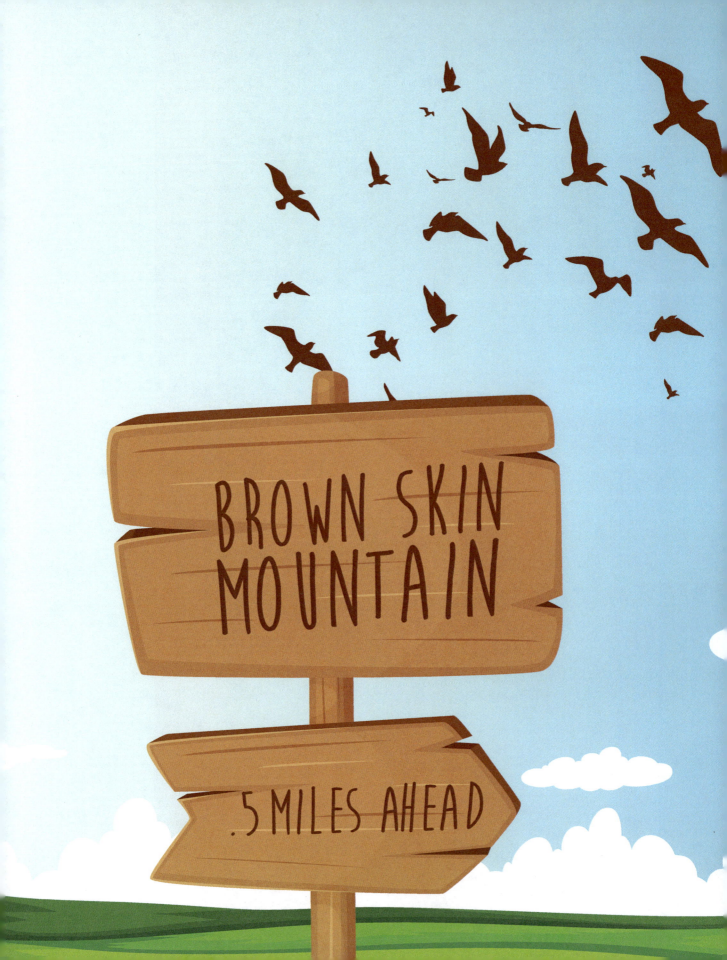

YOUR BROWN SKIN CREATES MELODIES
THAT ARE SUNG FROM THE TOPS OF MOUNTAINS,
MAKING THE BIRDS FLY
AND SENDING WATER TO THE FOUNTAINS.

YOUR DREADS AND BRAIDS,
THE PUDGE OF YOUR NOSE,
THE PLUMP IN YOUR LIPS,
AND YOUR CURLY AFRO.

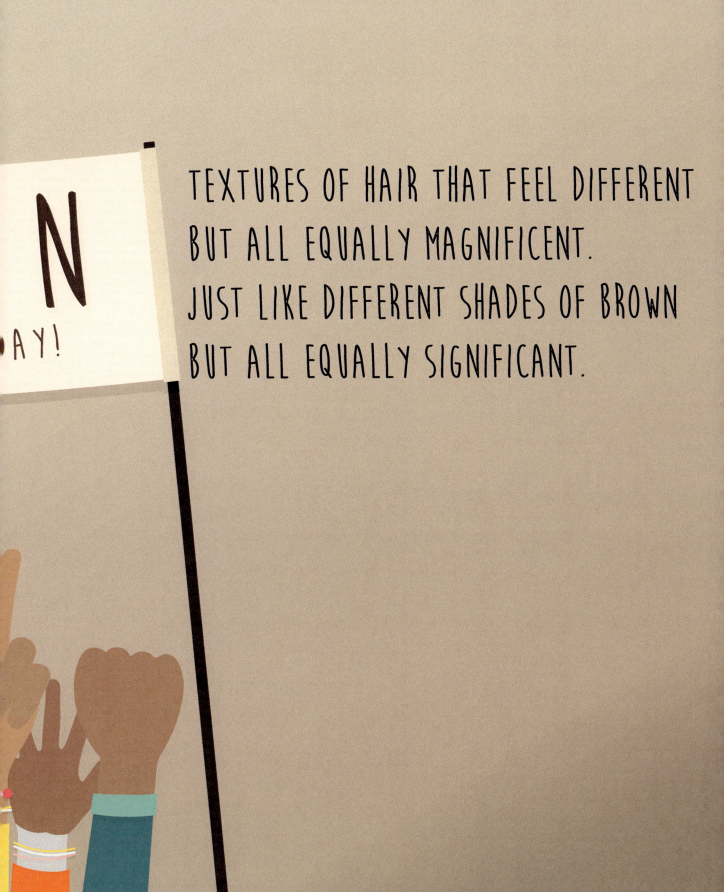

TEXTURES OF HAIR THAT FEEL DIFFERENT
BUT ALL EQUALLY MAGNIFICENT.
JUST LIKE DIFFERENT SHADES OF BROWN
BUT ALL EQUALLY SIGNIFICANT.

THE MOST BEAUTIFUL FLOWER COULD NEVER COMPARE TO YOU, SO CELEBRATE YOUR SKIN AND YOUR HAIR TOO.

BROWN SKIN, BROWN SKIN,
YOU DANCE TO THE CLUMP
AND THUMP OF A DRUM,
BUT THE BEAT OF YOUR HEART
IS WHERE YOUR RHYTHM COMES FROM.

Have faith and be brave,
love who you are.
Stay true to yourself
and you will go far."

FROM CONFIDENCE TO THE TRUTH,
AND THE ABILITY TO WIN,
EVERYTHING YOU'LL NEED
IS FOUND FROM WITHIN.

Made in the USA
Monee, IL
02 April 2022